W9-AWA-234

D⸱

MAI 2 0 2001

Pigs

by Peter Brady

Bridgestone Books

an Imprint of Capstone Press

Bridgestone Books are published by Capstone Press
818 North Willow Street, Mankato, Minnesota 56001
Copyright © 1996 by Capstone Press
All rights reserved
Printed in the United States of America

Library of Congress Cataloging-in-Publication Data
Brady, Peter. 1944–
    Pigs/Peter Brady
    p. cm.
    Includes bibliographical references and index.
    Summary: Introduces pigs by describing their physical characteristics, where they live,
    what they eat, their special skills, and what they provide for people.
    ISBN 1-56065-345-0
    1. Swine--Juvenile literature. [1. Pigs.] I. Title.
SF395.5.B735 1996
630.4--dc20

                                    95-54165
                                      CIP
                                       AC

Photo credits
William Muñoz: cover, 4, 8-10, 18-20
Lynn M. Stone: 6, 12-16

William Muñoz is a freelance photographer. He has a B.A. from the
University of Montana. He has taken photographs for many children's books.
William and his wife live on a farm near St. Ignatius, Montana, where they
raise cattle and horses.

Table of Contents

Words in **boldface** type in the text are defined in the Words to Know section in the back of this book.

What Is a Pig?

A pig is a farm animal. Pigs are raised for food or to breed more pigs. A male pig is called a boar. A female pig is called a sow.

What Pigs Look Like

Pigs have round bodies, short legs, and a curly tail. They can be black, white, tan, or spotted. A full-grown pig usually weighs 800 pounds (360 kilograms).

Where Pigs Live

Pigs live on farms. Most pigs are kept inside barns. They usually have an outside pen with feeding **troughs** and a cooling mud hole.

What Pigs Eat

Most pigs are fed grain and water, but they will eat almost anything. They will eat meat, vegetables, bread, and family leftovers. They can **digest** things humans cannot, such as grass and roots.

Special Skills

Pigs are considered the smartest farm animals. They can be taught to roll over, fetch, race, and dance. They have a sharp sense of smell and can find things underground with their snout.

Mud

Pigs lie in the mud to keep cool and wet. They get hot because they do not sweat like humans do. They can get sunburned because they do not have much hair.

What Pigs Give Us

Bacon, ham, sausage, and pork chops come from pigs. Their skin is also used to make leather for gloves, shoes, and other things. Doctors can save lives by replacing bad human heart **valves** with valves from pig hearts.

Hands On: Make a Piggy Bank

To make a piggy bank, you will need a clean one-gallon (3.8-liter) jug, four small paper cups, pink felt, one pink pipe cleaner, and glue.

1. Turn the jug on its side. The cap of the jug will be the pig's snout. The handle should be on top.
2. Glue the four cups to the bottom of the jug. These are the pig's legs.
3. Cut the felt into triangles. Glue them to the top of the jug. These are the pig's ears.
4. Have an adult poke a small hole in the back of the jug. Push the pipe cleaner through the hole and twist it into a curl. This is the pig's tail.
5. Draw eyes on the jug with a marker.
6. Remove the cap when you want to put coins in your piggy bank.

Words to Know

breed—group of animals that come from the same ancestors

digest—to change food into something the body can use

trough—long, narrow container used to hold food or water

valve—little flap that regulates the flow of blood

Read More

Fowler, Allan. *If It Weren't For Farmers*. Chicago: Children's Press, 1993.

Fowler, Allan. *Smart, Clean Pigs*. Chicago: Children's Press, 1993.

Gibbons, Gail. *Farming*. New York: Holiday House, 1988.

King-Smith, Dick. *All Pigs are Beautiful*. Cambridge, Mass.: Candlewick Press, 1993.

Index